Evernote: The Missing Manual

Getting the Most out of Evernote

by Tammy Clevenger

December, 2013

Organize Your Life

Congratulations! You have made the decision to learn more about Evernote, possibly the most effective personal and business information management tool you will ever use.

To the inexperienced user, Evernote appears to be a simplistic note-taking application. However, Evernote is so much more. Index and organize every aspect of your life with Evernote. You can create notes that contain images, text and links to web pages and documents. Use tags to make your notes searchable and embed links to other notes inside your notes. Access Evernote from any Internet-connected configured device.

With Evernote, your information follows you wherever you go. Evernote provides a cross-platform solution for organizing all of your business and personal data. Learn to use Evernote effectively to increase your productivity and ensure that you will never again lose an important resource, forget a birthday or misplace a to-do list.

I. Evernote Overview

The Evernote suite of applications is a multi-platform, cloud-based storage solution for capturing and storing data. Your data is indexed and searchable from any device that is configured for use with Evernote.

Create an account to capture and store text notes, images, web pages, voice recordings and more. when you save an Evernote note, the content automatically becomes indexed and searchable. Additionally, you can access your Evernote notes and notebooks from any device or location. Evernote data is transmitted over an SSL connection, so the data is encrypted during transfer. However, if you store sensitive information, you can encrypt text blocks to ensure that your data is safe, even if someone gains unauthorized access to one or more of your devices.

II. Evernote Features

A. Notes

Notes are the building blocks of Evernote. Notes can consist of text memos, audio recordings, photos, web pages, documents, videos and other files. You can set reminders on notes, and track the notes to completion in the Evernote application.

B. Cloud-Based

Evernote data is stored in the cloud and accessible from any Internet-connected device. Use the desktop application to capture and create notes on your PC or Mac. Use the mobile app to generate notes from your smartphone or tablet. You can even access your cloud storage from the Evernote site if no configured devices are available. Just open the site and log in with your Evernote credentials.

C. Integrates with All Devices

Your Evernote notes are stored in the cloud and available to all configured devices in real time. If you create a note on your phone, the note is immediately sync'ed with your computer and other devices. You must manually sync from the desktop application.

D. Powerful Search Feature

Evernote includes a powerful search feature that quickly and efficiently locates notes containing searched tags or keywords. Use tags and notebooks to categorize and organize your notes.

E. Notes vs. Notebooks

When you first start using Evernote, the most challenging task will likely be deciding when to create a single note versus a notebook. Create a single note for a small amount of information that will only be infrequently modified, if edited at all. For example, store your warranty information for your appliances in a single note. Create notebooks when you intend to perform ongoing additions and edits to the content. When researching a topic for an article, create a notebook to contain all relevant resources, web clips, images and data.

F. Email Notes

When you create an Evernote account, an Email Notes account is also created for you. Locate your Email Notes account in the Account Info section of the Evernote desktop application. The email address will consist of your username plus several random characters, appended with "@m.evernote.com."

G. Tweet Notes

You can also send notes to your Evernote platform from Twitter. Just tweet your note to "@MyEV." Your note appears in all of your Evernote apps, and in your Twitter timeline.

H. Sharing Features

You can share your notes with other users, even with the free plan. Upgrade to the Premium plan to give other users Edit access to your notes.

I. OCR

For mobile devices that support Optical Character Recognition, or "OCR," Evernote will identify and index text characters in images. For example, if you snap a photo of yourself standing next to a boat named "Little Sally," Evernote's OCR feature will index "Little Sally" so the note can be found when this keyword phrase is searched.

III. Evernote Plans and Limits

A. Free and Premium Plans

Use the basic Evernote service free of charge. However, you can also purchase a Premium or Business plan to enjoy additional features. The free plan includes 60 MB per month data limit. Monitor usage with the Usage Meter in the Account Info dialog box in the desktop application. When you purchase the Premium version for a nominal fee, the monthly data limit increases to 1, 024 MB. Both the free and Premium plans are limited to a total of 250 notebooks and 100,000 notes.

B. Free vs. Premium: Plan Differences

With the free plan, you can share your Evernote notebooks with other users, but those users cannot edit your notebooks. With the Premium plan, you can grant users Edit privileges for your notebooks. At the time of this writing, the Premium plan is priced at $5 per month.

C. Evernote for Business

Evernote for Business offers an inexpensive, centralized collaboration solution for teams. The cost of Evernote for Business is $10 per user, per month. With Evernote for Business, users create Business Notebooks and share information in Related Notes. Tag Related Notes with applicable keywords to track knowledge and input from the team on each project.

The Evernote for Business dashboard enables managers and team leaders to view and edit users from the People view. Find out what the team is working on and the knowledge in transfer by viewing each team member's profile. Join applicable notebooks and limit access to others from the dashboard.

Users can convert personal notebooks to Business Notebooks with a click of the mouse or a tap of the screen. Open a note to view other users who have access to the content. Evernote for Business also integrates with existing directory management systems for programmatic control over user accounts.

D. Evernote for Salesforce

The Evernote for Business subscription can be applied to the Evernote for Salesforce module. This module provides seamless integration between the Salesforce and Evernote platforms. Create and share notes with the team right from the Salesforce interface.

IV. Evernote Installation and Setup

To fully utilize Evernote and all of its features, set up the platform on all your computers and mobile devices. To link your devices in the cloud, you will need to create an Evernote account.

A. Evernote Account

The first step in setting up Evernote is creating an Evernote account. You can set up an Evernote account by browsing to the website and completing the New Account form. However, you can also create a new account when you first open either the desktop application or the mobile app. Create an Evernote account using any available method, then log in with the new account credentials to set up Evernote. You will then log into the same account from each device from which you will use Evernote.

B. Evernote Mobile App

1. Mobile App Versions

The free Evernote mobile app is available for iOS and Android operating systems. In addition, the Evernote app is available for BlackBerry, WebOS, Windows Mobile, Windows 8 for touchscreens and the Google Wave operating systems. However, the iOS and Android versions are the two versions that represent the most market share for the app.

a. Install iOS App

To obtain Evernote for the iPad, iPhone or iPod Touch, open the App Store on the device and search for "Evernote." Tap the entry for the app in the search results to view the app details page. Tap the "Free" icon. The Apple ID prompt displays. Type your Apple ID and password to download and install the app. You can also download and install the app to your device using iTunes.

b. Install Android App

To get the Android version of Evernote, tap the "Play" icon in the Android Applications screen to open the Google Play Store app. Tap the "Apps" icon, then type "Evernote" in the Search bar. Tap the "Evernote" entry in the search results to open the details page, then tap "Install." A list of permissions that the app must be granted appears on the screen. Tap "Accept" to grant permissions to the app. Evernote is downloaded and installed on your Android device.

When you first open the Evernote app on an Android device, you are prompted to link the app to the same primary Google account you use for your phone. If you don't want to link to the Google account, you can create a new Evernote account with a non-Gmail email address. Note that you will likely store sensitive, personal information in Evernote. For security purposes, consider instead creating a stand-alone account for Evernote that is not linked to a free, cloud-based email service that scans your messages.

2. Create Your First Note

When you first launch the mobile app, prompts guide you through the process of creating your first note. Tap the "New Note" icon in the Setup wizard to see a sample to-do list. Use the sample list as a guide for creating your first check list.

a. The Formatting Toolbar

The New Note form includes the Formatting toolbar. Use the tools in the toolbar to format the text in your notes. The toolbar includes the Bold, Italics and Underline tools, as well as Bulleted and Unbulleted List tools and the Check Box control. Tap the "Arrow" icon to collapse and reveal the toolbar. Tap and hold the "Check Mark" in the upper left corner of the New Note form to return to the Evernote main screen.

b. The Check Box Control

The sample check list implements the check box control, which you can use when creating your own lists and notes. Tap inside an note, then tap the "Check Box" icon in the Formatting toolbar to place a check box in the note. Type the label for the item, then save the note. Press "Enter" to move to the next line item. The second check box automatically appears in the note. Use the check box to check completed items off your to-do lists. Compose the remainder of the list, then when you are ready to save the note, tap the "Menu" button in the top toolbar. Tap "Save." The note is saved and indexed in the Evernote database.

c. Add Multimedia

You can add audio files and photos to Evernote notes. Tap the "Camera" icon in the top toolbar of the New Note form to launch your Camera app. Snap one or more photos. The photos are automatically inserted into the open note. Tap the "Paper Clip" icon to attach an audio or document file. Tap the "Check Mark" in the top toolbar to set a reminder for the note, and tap the "Alarm Clock" icon to mark the item as "Done," clear the reminder or set a due date for the note.

d. Add Tags

Tags help you quickly find data in the Evernote app with the Search feature. Tags are optional, and if you use them, you must specify tags that work for you. For example, if you plan to manage your children's information in Evernote, tag each note pertaining to a particular child with a keyword containing the child's name. The more effectively you apply tags, the easier your information will be to find when you need it.

To apply tags to a note, open the note for editing, then tap the "Menu" icon in the New Note form. Tap the "Tags" option to open the Choose Tags screen. Tap the "Add Tags.." field, then type the first tag for the note. Tap "OK" to save the tag. The tag displays at the top of the Choose Tags screen. To delete a tag, tap the "X" on the right side of the Tag label. Tap the "Select Personal Tags" link to choose tags you have used in other notes.

e. Create a Notebook

Create notebooks to organize notes with similar topics and themes. For example, if you use Evernote to organize marketing projects, you can create a notebook for each client, each project or each department you manage. If you manage your family's information in Evernote, create a notebook for each member of the family. Define the organizational schema that works best for you. After all, you will only get the most out of Evernote if you become a regular user. Use a structure that represents how you organize your business or lifestyle when setting up your Evernote notebooks so your transition to Evernote to manage your life's data is a smooth one.

To create a notebook, tap the "Menu" icon in the New Note form, then tap "Notebook." A list of your available notebooks opens. Tap the "+" icon in the upper right corner of the Choose Notebook screen to open the New Notebook form. Type a name for the new notebook in the Name field, then tap "OK."

That's it! Your new notebook is created and saved. Now, you can move your existing notes to the applicable notebook, and then assign new notes to notebooks as you create them going forward. After you finish setting up the app, then creating your first note and notebook, you can close the note and exit the app. The next time you launch the app, you will see the Evernote Main Screen.

3. The Evernote Mobile App Main Screen

Think of the Evernote Main Screen as your Evernote central dashboard. All of your notes, notebooks, tags and accounts are available at the touch of the screen. You will find four icons for features you will frequently use, along with a list of tabs for accessing your stored data.

a. Icons

Tap the "New Note" icon to open the new form to create a new note. Tap the "Camera" icon to launch your camera app and snap a shot on the go. Tap the "Microphone" icon to launch the voice recorder app to record a voice note. Tap the "Image" icon to open your Camera Roll or Photo Gallery to attach an image to a note.

b.Tabs

You will find several tabs on the Evernote main screen to quickly access your Notes, Notebooks, Tags and other features. The tabs also include the number of items in the category. For example, if you have created 5 notes, you'll see the number "5" on the Notes tab in the Evernote main screen.

c. Evernote Mobile App Settings

1. Settings Menu

You can configure a few application-specific settings in the Evernote mobile app. Tap the "Menu" icon in the New Note form, then tap "Settings" to open the app Settings menu. You can enable "Use GPS Satellites" to obtain your location information from GPS satellites. However, note that enabling this feature increases the drain on your device battery.

Tap the "Use Wireless Networks" to instruct Evernote to use wireless networks for uploading and interacting with data in the cloud. Enable this feature to save minutes on your cellular plan. Enable the "Auto-Title" option to allow Evernote to automatically assign a title to notes based on the content. Enable the "Activate Multi-Shot Camera" option if your device camera does not have the multi-shot feature by default. Once you have enabled the desired features, tap the "Back" arrow to save the settings and return to the app.

2. Set Location

If you do not have Location Services enabled on your mobile device, you can manually configure your location in Evernote. If Location Services are enabled, your location is automatically updated in the app. To manually set your location in the Evernote app, tap the "Menu" icon in the New Note form, then tap "Set Location." Tap your location on the map, then tap "Done" to save your location. When the Location setting is configured, your notes are automatically tagged with geolocation tags.

C. Evernote Desktop Application

The desktop version of Evernote is available for both Windows and Mac operating systems. Both versions are free and can be downloaded from the Evernote site. Download and install Evernote to your computer, then launch the application to run the Setup wizard. The first task in the wizard is to create your Evernote account or log in with existing credentials.

Once you are logged in to the platform, the Evernote desktop software opens and your desktop dashboard displays. From your dashboard, you can create notes and notebooks, add tags and attach files from your computer to your notes.

1. Desktop Features

The desktop application includes basically the same features as the mobile app. Use the desktop version of Evernote when you want to capture web pages while surfing the Web on your laptop or desktop machine. However, the desktop application differs in one way from the mobile app. You must click the "Sync" button in the top navigation bar to sync your notes from the desktop application to the cloud. When you use the Evernote mobile app, your notes automatically sync to the cloud.

The desktop application also includes the "Activity" tab located in the top navigation bar. Click this tab to see all of the latest activity on your Evernote account.

2. Email Integration

When you install the desktop version of Evernote on a computer with Microsoft Outlook installed, the Evernote add-in is automatically installed to the email client. Evernote offers an add-in for Mozilla Thunderbird, but you must download the plug-in from the Evernote site.

3. Create a New Note

Open the New Note form in the desktop application by clicking the "File" option in the top navigation menu, then clicking the "New Note" option. The New Note form opens in the center panel of Evernote. Type a title in the Name field, if desired, then type a note or drag and drop photos or files from your computer into the New Note form. You will not find a "Save" button. Your notes are automatically saved locally as you create them. Click "Sync" to sync your notes to the cloud.

You can also click the "File" option in the top navigation menu, then select "New Note book," "New Tag" or "New Saved Search" to create any of these Evernote elements. Click the "Import" option to import Microsoft OneNote files or Evernote files from an external source

D. Evernote Web Clipper Add-On

The Evernote Web Clipper add-on integrates with your Firefox, Opera or Google Chrome browser to capture web pages and clippings that can stored in the cloud with your notes. Web Clipper is also available for the Safari browser for Mac. Download the add-on from the Evernote Web Clipper site and install the software on your desktop computer. Close, then reopen your browser to activate and the tool. Surf the Web, then when you find web pages you want to save, capture the page as an Evernote note with the Web Clipper tool.

The Web Clipper tool appears and behaves differently depending on which browser you are using, but the concept of clipping involves highlighting a block of text, then clicking the "Web Clipper" button in the browser toolbar to clip the page. In Internet Explorer, right-click on the highlighted text to select the Web Clipper tool.

Annotate and highlight the web clippings before saving the note and indexing the clippings in the app. The content of the clippings becomes searchable once saved in the app.

V. Using Evernote

To get the most out of all the features of Evernote, you must develop your own personal strategy for using the platform. If you are a student, you can quickly adapt Evernote to capture written, typed and audio class notes. Attach tags to your notes, then sort them into notebooks to organize your life. Use Evernote to organize your clients or projects on the job, but don't stop there. Evernote is the perfect digital filing cabinet for household records and personal memos.

A. School

To use Evernote for school, create a notebook for each of your classes. If you are conducting a research project, such as researching a topic for an article, create a notebook for the project, then store your applicable notes in the notebook.

B. On the Job

Create a notebook for each prospect, client, project or meeting to keep track of your notes on the job. Record audio highlights of meetings, then add tags to make your audio notes searchable. Snap photos, then annotate the images prior to sharing them with your team.

C. At Home

Create a notebook for each member of the family, then tag individual notes with specific categories. For example, little Mary's notebook might contain her report cards, school records, after-school sports paperwork and birthday wish list. You can create a notebook for household records, and another to track your vehicle records. Scan your receipts and paperwork for large purchases using your OCR-enabled mobile device, then the items become searchable in the Evernote database.

VI. Productivity Tips and Tricks

How many times have you composed a to-do list, only to misplace the list? With Evernote, your to-do lists, notes to yourself, research clips, recipes and any other data you capture in your notes are stored in one location. Increase your productivity by organizing your notes into organically-themed notebooks. Use tags in your notes, but not so many that you can't remember them when you need to find information. Cross-tag notes, when applicable, to find pertinent information when you need it. Think of Evernote as your all-in-one personal filing system that you can use for nearly any purpose, from any device in nearly any location.

A. Useful Tips

1. Create an Inbox

Create an Inbox notebook, particularly if you plan to tweet or email your notes to your account. Name the notebook "_INBOX" so the notebook displays at the top of your Notebooks list. Set the Inbox notebook as your default notebook so your emailed and tweeted notes are automatically routed to this notebook.

2. Master Search Syntax

You can specify precise saved searches with Evernote's search syntax. To search your notes for a specific tag, type "tag:" followed by the tag to locate. For example, to find all notes tagged with the keyword "Ernesto," type "tag:Ernesto" in the search field.

You can also append the search term with the approximate or specific Created Date. To search for all notes tagged with the keyword "Ernesto" created last week, type "tag:Ernesto created: week-1."

3. Note Links

Note Links are links you can create in your notes that refer to information in other notes. Note Links are simply hyperlinks in notes. In the desktop application, just right-click on a note, then click "Copy Note Link" to copy the link to your clipboard. Open the destination note, then paste the link in the desired location within the content.

4. The Evernote Toolbar

For notes that you open frequently, create an icon on the Evernote toolbar for the note. Simply drag and drop the note onto the toolbar to create the icon. Click the icon to quickly open the note from anywhere in the app.

B. Case Studies in Productivity

1. The Author

One prolific author on the West coast uses Evernote to organize and construct her lengthier articles and books. She first creates a notebook, then creates an outline for the project in a note. She researches her topic, capturing web pages with the Web Clipper, and then inserting the clips in the appropriate sections of the outline. She fleshes out the sections with content, images and multimedia, then pulls it all together in a first draft. After a few reviews and rewrites, the piece is complete. All of her research, notes and work product are included in the Evernote notebook. She can access her work from any location using any one of her several devices.

2. The Property Manager

A busy property manager in Houston uses Evernote to organize and manage rental properties for his clients. He creates an Evernote notebook for each property to track tenants contact information and payment history, maintenance and repair tasks, vendor information and property records for each property. He recently discovered a property in bad shape after a tenant moved out. He was able to snap several photos of the damage, forward the photos to the property owner and schedule a clean-up crew in a matter of minutes - all with the help of Evernote.

3. The Soccer Mom

The Soccer Mom in Chicago uses Evernote for everything from keeping up with her children's ballet classes and baseball practices to storing shopping lists and recipes. She coordinates menus by creating her shopping lists when she plans meals for the week on Sunday evening. She simply takes her smartphone to the supermarket, walks the aisles and checks each item off her grocery list as she places them in the cart. When she sees a new product that she wants to know more about, she can research the product on the Web while in the store, then save the web page in the appropriate notebook.

VII. Safety and Security

The Evernote platform has its limitations when it comes to storing sensitive data. Though your notes are encrypted during data transfer, the content is not encrypted on the server. Moreover, if you have Evernote installed on your mobile device, and your device is lost or stolen, all of your Evernote data on all of your devices is compromised. You can, however, encrypt blocks of text within a note.

A. Encrypt Text

To encrypt text within a note, highlight the text, then right-click or tap and hold to display the context menu. Click or tap the "Encrypt Selected Text" option. The Note Encryption dialog box opens. Type, then retype a password for the encrypted text. You can also specify a question or prompt for the password. Click or tap the "Remember Password Until I Quit Evernote" option to keep the encrypted text visible while you have the Evernote app open. If you don't check this option, the encrypted text is masked. Click or tap "OK" to save the settings. Note that you cannot encrypt an entire Evernote note, nor can you encrypt images or attachments.

B. What Not to Include in a Note

Do not store sensitive information, such as social security numbers, private medical records, bank account and credit card numbers, account passwords, home alarm codes, network SSIDs and passwords or any other data that, if compromised, presents a threat to your safety or the safety of your family.

VIII. Additional Evernote Applications

Evernote integrates with several complementary applications, such as Evernote Food and Hello, Skitch and Penultimate. Evernote Food is an application geared toward saving recipes and tracking meals. Hello provides an application to help you remember people. Skitch is a versatile annotation app and Penultimate is a handwriting app that enables you to draw elegant lettering on a mobile device or touch screen tablet.

Evernote Clean cleans up web pages and posts to make them more legible in a note, and Evernote Peek is a study tool that utilizes the iPad Smart Cover feature. All Evernote applications seamlessly integrate with one another and all apps utilize your Evernote account in the cloud.

IX. In Conclusion...

Evernote can be used to organize and manage practically every aspect of your life. The Evernote platform centralizes your to do lists, notes, Web bookmarks, photos and other information into a searchable database that you can access from any device. However, Evernote is only as useful as you make it. Using Evernote to its fullest can improve productivity and help you organize your life.

References and Resources

Evernote: Evernote Support

http://evernote.com/contact/support/

Evernote: Getting Started with Evernote

https://evernote.com/getting_started/

Evernote: Evernote Products

http://evernote.com/products/

Evernote: Web Clipper

http://evernote.com/webclipper/guide/